SHARKS
Voracious Hunters of the Sea

by Isidro Sánchez
Illustrated by Gabriel Casadevall and Ali Garousi

Gareth Stevens Publishing
MILWAUKEE

For a free color catalog describing Gareth Stevens' list of high-quality books,
call 1-800-542-2595 (USA) or 1-800-461-9120 (Canada).
Gareth Stevens' Fax: (414) 225-0377.

The editor would like to extend special thanks to Jan W. Rafert, Curator of Primates
and Small Mammals, Milwaukee County Zoo, Milwaukee, Wisconsin,
for his kind and professional help with the information in this book.

Library of Congress Cataloging-in-Publication Data

Sánchez, Isidro.
    [Tiburón. English]
    Sharks: voracious hunters of the sea / by Isidro Sánchez; illustrated by Gabriel
Casadevall and Ali Garousi.
       p. cm. — (Secrets of the animal world)
    Includes bibliographical references (p.) and index.
    Summary: Provides detailed descriptions of the physical characteristics and behavior
of sharks.
    ISBN 0-8368-1396-0 (lib. bdg.)
    1. Sharks—Juvenile literature. [1. Sharks.] I. Casadevall, Gabriel, ill. II. Garousi,
Ali, ill. III. Title. IV. Series.
QL638.9.S3513 1996
597'.31—dc20   95-45799

This North American edition first published in 1996 by
Gareth Stevens Publishing
1555 North RiverCenter Drive, Suite 201
Milwaukee, Wisconsin 53212 USA

This U.S. edition © 1996 by Gareth Stevens, Inc. Created with original © 1993
Ediciones Este, S.A., Barcelona, Spain. Additional end matter © 1996 by Gareth
Stevens, Inc.

Series editor: Patricia Lantier-Sampon
Editorial assistants: Diane Laska, Rita Reitci, Derek Smith

Printed in the United States of America

1 2 3 4 5 6 7 8 9 99 98 97 96

CONTENTS

BIG AND POWERFUL SHARKS

In all the seas of the world

Sharks inhabit all the seas of the world, from icy polar waters to warm tropical seas. Some sharks swim close to the surface and are great hunters. Others live on the ocean floor and are harmless. Most sharks live in the sea, but some, such as the blacktip shark, sometimes visit river outlets. The bull shark (one of two known freshwater sharks) can travel up the Amazon River more than 1,865 miles (3,000 km) from the ocean.

Great hunters, such as the tiger shark (above), the great white, and the hammerhead shark, are notorious because of their vicious attacks against swimmers.

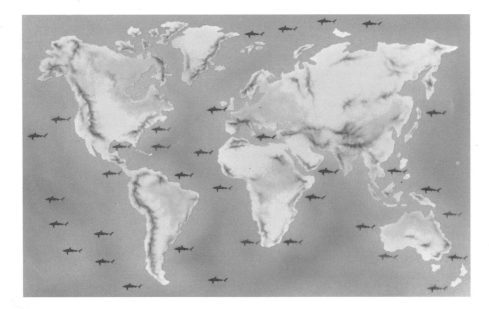

Sharks live in almost every sea and ocean in the world, although the most dangerous sharks are found in the warm waters of the tropics, close to the surface.

Feeding off the sea

Sunlight penetrates only a few feet (m) into the sea. Seaweed and plants live within these first few feet. These plants live off energy from sunlight. Millions of plant fragments float in the water, forming phytoplankton. This serves as food for zooplankton, tiny shrimps and baby fishes. Sardines and anchovies eat zooplankton; other fishes, such as tuna and cod, eat sardines and anchovies. Whales and some types of sharks just swim with their mouths open and scoop up tons of zooplankton. But the other sharks, the great carnivores of the sea, do not wait for their food to come to them. They hunt for it and use all their ferocity to find prey.

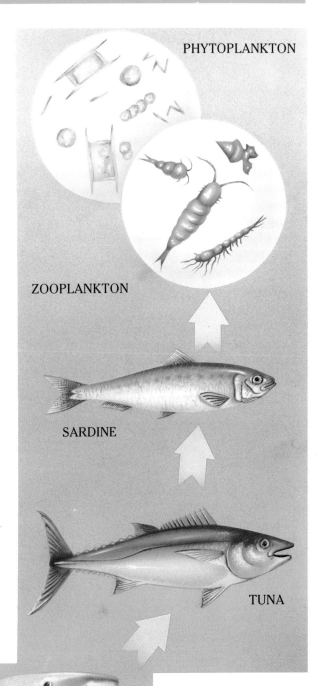

PHYTOPLANKTON

ZOOPLANKTON

SARDINE

TUNA

TIGER SHARK

This illustration shows one of the food chains of the sea, which ends with the great carnivores: the sharks.

Types of sharks

Sharks are fish, with a cartilage skeleton that is lighter and more flexible than bone. There are many types of sharks that feed on different kinds of food. Many sharks, such as the swell shark and the angel shark, live in the deepest oceans. Other sharks inhabiting the bottom of the sea are the sawshark with its long snout, and the sea fox with its enormous tail. Of the more than three hundred kinds of sharks, however, only about fifty are well known.

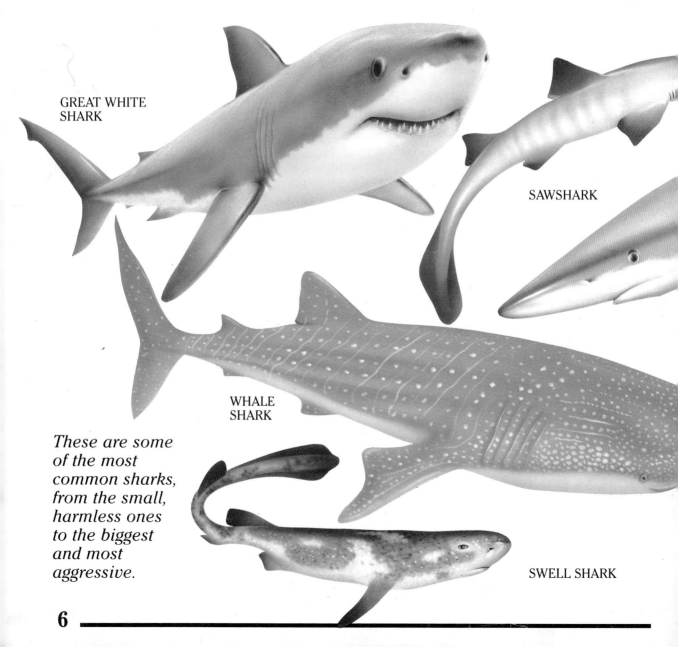

GREAT WHITE SHARK

SAWSHARK

WHALE SHARK

These are some of the most common sharks, from the small, harmless ones to the biggest and most aggressive.

SWELL SHARK

One of the largest and most notorious is the great white shark, which can grow to 33 feet (10 m) long. The tiger shark and the blacktip shark are also great hunters. The hammerhead shark, as its name suggests, has a hammer-shaped head.

The Galápagos shark lives in coral reefs, which it uses as a hiding place.

The shape of a shark's tail is ideal for chasing prey. But some sharks' tails have other uses; for example, the sea fox uses its tail to smack its prey.

BLACKTIP
SHARK

HAMMERHEAD
SHARK

ANGEL SHARK

TIGER SHARK
TAIL

SEA FOX
TAIL

GREAT WHITE
SHARK TAIL

INSIDE THE SHARK

This illustration shows what the inside of a shark looks like. The shark has a fusiform, or torpedo-shaped, body that is perfect for swimming fast to catch its prey.

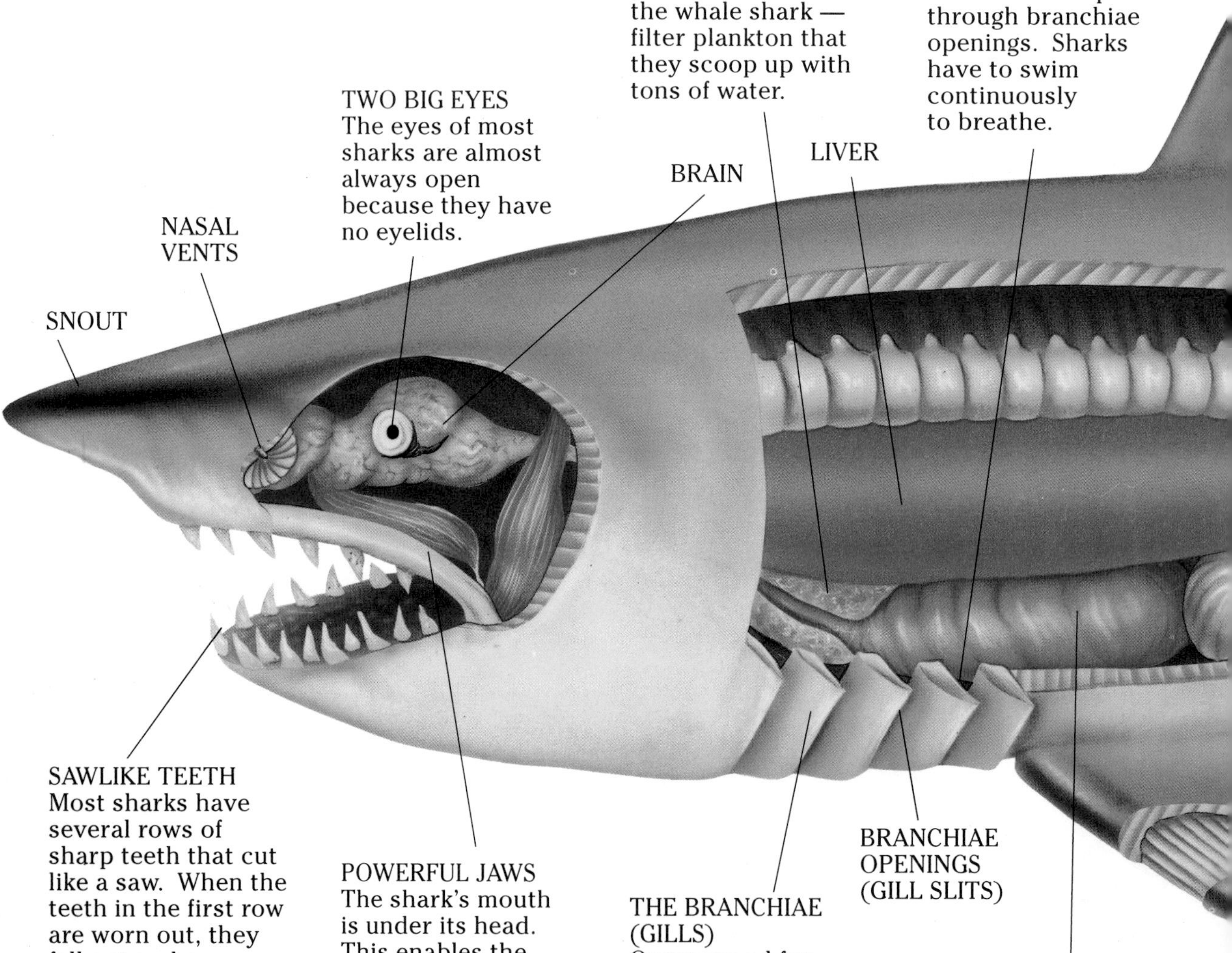

WHAT SHARKS EAT
Small sharks eat small fish. Big sharks eat big fish, seals, and dolphins. The two biggest sharks — the basking shark and the whale shark — filter plankton that they scoop up with tons of water.

HOW SHARKS BREATHE
When sharks swim, water goes into the branchiae. When the oxygen dissolved in the water has reached the blood, the water is expelled through branchiae openings. Sharks have to swim continuously to breathe.

TWO BIG EYES
The eyes of most sharks are almost always open because they have no eyelids.

NASAL VENTS

SNOUT

BRAIN

LIVER

SAWLIKE TEETH
Most sharks have several rows of sharp teeth that cut like a saw. When the teeth in the first row are worn out, they fall out and are replaced by the next row.

POWERFUL JAWS
The shark's mouth is under its head. This enables the jaws to open much wider to trap prey.

THE BRANCHIAE (GILLS)
Organs used for breathing. Blood absorbs oxygen from water in the branchiae.

BRANCHIAE OPENINGS (GILL SLITS)

STOMACH

A SILENT
"NAVIGATIONAL"
SYSTEM
The shark's skin is
covered with sharp
scales that channel
the water to propel
the shark forward.
This enables the
shark to glide
silently through
the water.

PROPULSION FORCE
The caudal fin is the
shark's tail. It is used
to beat the water to
move the shark
forward. It also
works like a rudder;
when the shark wants
to change direction,
it bends the fin to
one side.

DORSAL FINS
These fins help steer
the shark in the
direction it wants
to go. Most sharks
have two dorsal fins.

DIGESTIVE SYSTEM
The shark chews its
prey into small pieces
that are then broken
down by gastric
juices. The nutrients
are absorbed by the
intestine.

VERTEBRAL
COLUMN

CAUDAL
FIN

ANAL
FIN

INTESTINE

PELVIC FIN

STABILIZERS
The shark has two
pectoral fins and two
pelvic fins. These
help the shark
maintain its balance
while it swims. They
also help it go up,
down, or sideways in
the water.

PECTORAL
FIN

GREAT HUNTERS OF THE SEA

Ready to hunt

Sharks possess remarkable detection systems. One of the most important is its sense of smell. The shark's smell membranes are sensitive to substances dissolved in water, such as blood from a wounded fish. Another system is the lateral line, or "sixth sense," that the shark uses to pick up waves caused by movement. The shark can also detect the electricity all moving animals produce. Small charges are transmitted through water and received by sensory detectors called ampullae of Lorenzini.

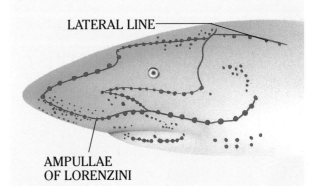

LATERAL LINE

AMPULLAE
OF LORENZINI

The lateral line extends from the head to the tail. It has many nerve endings that detect the movement of waves in the water.

Through pores in the skin, the ampullae of Lorenzini "inform" the shark that there is a creature nearby.

AMPULLAE OF
LORENZINI

NASAL
VENTS

Smell is one of the shark's most important senses for catching prey.

SMELL
MEMBRANES

Tracking and attacking

Sharks usually swim around in circles without a specific route. They keep track of the smell and taste of the water. A shark detects the first sign of prey through sounds that echo in the water. The shark's acute sense of smell provides it with more information. Finally, the electric charges produced by the prey's movements help the shark pinpoint its precise position. Now the shark moves in for the kill. It closes its eyes and opens its enormous jaws. The shark bites into the prey with its lower jaw and rakes the prey into its mouth with the teeth of its movable upper jaw.

1. Sound waves in the water produced by moving prey attract the shark.

2. The shark picks up the prey's smell and moves silently and skillfully toward it.

3. The shark attacks — it opens its enormous jaws and takes the prey into its mouth.

that some fish get a "free" ride with sharks?

People once believed sharks had poor eyesight and that pilot fish guided them to their prey. In reality, pilot fish use sharks to get a free ride. They swim in large groups around the sharks, ride the strong currents, and travel at the same speed without any physical effort. By swimming this way, pilot fish don't even have to hunt for themselves. Sharks are messy eaters, and the pilot fish eat the remains of the shark's prey.

The shark's enemies

The shark's main enemy is very often another shark of a different species. The great hunters, such as the great white shark, hunt smaller and less aggressive sharks. Also, sharks of the same family attack each other: the biggest and strongest attack the smallest. But the shark's greatest enemy is the sperm whale. The shark also tends to avoid the seemingly harmless dolphin, although sharks sometimes follow a group of dolphins with the aim of catching a young one that gets left behind.

Sharks often bite each other while attacking their prey.

A dolphin can defeat a shark in combat. If the dolphin encounters a shark, it can drive its head into the shark's stomach — the most vulnerable part of its body — and injure the shark with its sharp snout.

Danger on the beach!

Despite the notoriety they have gained, most sharks are not dangerous to humans. The few dangerous species attack between fifty and seventy-five times each year. This is a low figure if we consider the number of bathers that swim in shark-infested waters.

Most shark attacks against humans happen in the waters off the coasts of Australia, southern Africa, and the Caribbean. Many of these attacks are due to

Surfers in some parts of the world need to be on the lookout for sharks.

To protect bathers, anti-shark nets are placed where sharks are known to swim.

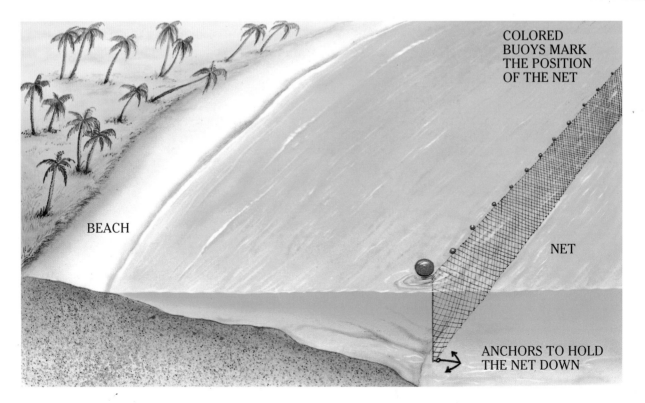

COLORED BUOYS MARK THE POSITION OF THE NET

BEACH

NET

ANCHORS TO HOLD THE NET DOWN

solitary sharks that approach the beaches. They attack surfers or bathers who have swum out too far from the coast. The same shark can attack several times on the same day. Having successfully attacked its prey, a shark may return for another attack. At beaches where sharks are spotted frequently, nets are installed to prevent the sharks from approaching the shore and attacking bathers.

The great white and the mako (below) are two sharks that often attack humans.

A quiet and peaceful life

Many sharks are small and harmless. The sharks that live at the bottom of the sea — such as the angel shark — spend most of their time resting. Some sharks don't even have to hunt for prey. They lay in wait on the bottom, camouflaged, until their prey approaches. The bamboo shark sucks prey off the bottom of the sea like a vacuum cleaner. Other small and harmless sharks live off tiny fishes, mollusks, sea urchins, and other marine life.

Many sharks, such as this Port Jackson shark, live a peaceful life at the bottom of the sea by feeding off invertebrates like sea urchins.

The bamboo shark has a mouth that works like a vacuum cleaner. It covers cracks and holes on the seabed and sucks the contents into its mouth.

that the great white is the most dangerous shark in the world?

Many poisonous animals, such as cobras, have attacked humans. Great carnivores, such as tigers and bears, have also attacked humans. But none is as feared as the great white shark. With its 33-foot (10 m)-long body, sharp teeth, and dorsal fin cutting the water's surface, it is the terror of the seas. The great white shark is nature's most efficient killing machine.

HOW SHARKS LIVE

A solitary hunter

Sharks cover great distances to find and catch their prey, and they almost always hunt alone. When they travel with other members of their family, they divide into small groups, and each one follows a different lead to possible prey. When they find their prey, they come together again for the attack. The shark doesn't attack only when it is hungry. It can also attack when it is frightened or when it feels trapped. On such occasions, it normally tries to escape.

Although dangerous, the blacktip shark seldom attacks humans.

The blacktip shark eats the remains of food thrown into the sea from passing ships.

In search of a mate

In almost all sharks, there are noticeable differences between males and females. Females are often larger, and their teeth are not as pointed. Like many female and male animals, sharks look for a mate at a certain time of year: the courting period. When courting, the male shark shows it is stronger than other males by biting the female's loin.

Since the female is larger and has a thicker skin, these bites don't hurt; in fact, they are signs of affection.

The visible differences between male and female sharks is called dimorphism.

Learning to hunt

Many sharks that live on the sea bottom are oviparous — the females lay eggs. Unlike other species of fish, which lay thousands and even millions of eggs, the female shark lays only a few. But some female sharks that live in the open sea, such as the great hunters, give birth to live young that have hatched from eggs and have developed inside the mother. Newborn sharks already know how to swim and soon learn to hunt on their own. They must learn this as soon as possible to survive.

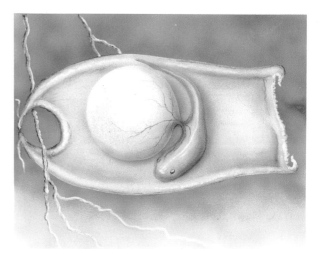

The oviparous shark's eggs are protected by a tough pouch attached to rocks or seaweed.

Some sharks give live birth in areas that are safe from hungry sharks.

that mechanical sharks were used during the shooting of the movie *Jaws*?

During the filming of the movie *Jaws* and its sequels, underwater cameramen and shark specialists spent months preparing the sharks in swimming pools. But for the starring great white shark, they built three mechanical sharks, bigger than the real one and with teeth twice as large as the real size. These mechanical sharks could be switched on as needed for filming.

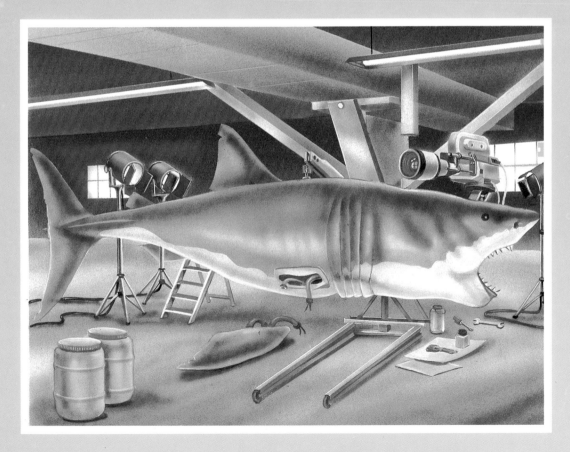

ANCESTORS OF THE SHARK

Fifty feet (15 m) long

Shark ancestors first appeared in Earth's oceans about 400 million years ago. Our human ancestors appeared 3 million years ago. Shark ancestors resembled today's sharks, but they were larger and more aggressive. They were called Hybodus and measured up to 50 feet (15 m) in length. Powerful 8-inch (20 cm)-long teeth were used to attack armored fish that inhabited the seas at that time.

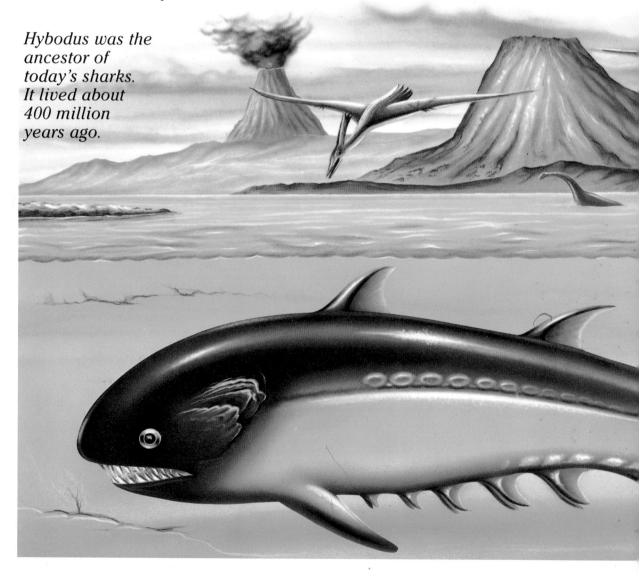

Hybodus was the ancestor of today's sharks. It lived about 400 million years ago.

Scientists know when and how the shark's ancestors lived because of fossils left by their teeth.

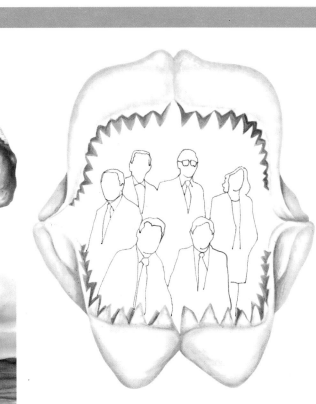

The enormous jaws of a Hybodus reconstructed from information provided by fossils.

Hybodus evolved over hundreds of millions of years until it reached the shapes of today's sharks. The appearance of the first sharks coincided with the disappearance of the great sea reptiles and, in their place, the first marine mammals appeared: the whales. This happened more than 150 million years ago, and sharks have hardly changed since that time.

APPENDIX TO

SHARKS
Voracious Hunters of the Sea

SHARK SECRETS

Shark's teeth. Some primitive cultures use shark teeth as ornaments and weapons.

▲ A terrible weapon. The sea fox shark lives in the deepest parts of the ocean and has a curious way of hunting. It stuns its prey by smacking them with its enormous tail and then eats them.

▲ A "midget" shark. The cigar shark is the smallest in the world. As an adult, it measures only 20 inches (50 cm).

▲ Seeing in all directions. The hammerhead shark's eyes are at each end of its head. This gives it a wide range of vision.

The giant shark. The whale shark is the biggest fish in the world. It can grow up to 60 feet (18 m) in length.

▶ **A shark attack.** On February 13, 1974, a fourteen-year-old Australian boy named Desmond Kendrick was attacked by a great white shark one morning when the anti-shark net was not installed. Amazingly, he only suffered wounds to the leg.

Film star. The great white shark, seen in many movies, is a "heavyweight" artist. It weighs around 8,820 pounds (4,000 kg) and measures up to 33 feet (10 m) in length.

1. Do sharks have several rows of teeth?
a) No.
b) Yes.
c) Yes, but only in the upper jaw.

2. What are branchiae?
a) A part of the shark's stomach.
b) Kind of plaques that cover the shark's skin.
c) Organs the shark has for breathing.

3. What is the lateral line?
a) A system for detecting prey.
b) The shark's spine.
c) A line over the shark's eyes.

4. How many shark attacks are there in the world every year?
a) About 50-75 a year.
b) More than 1,000 a year.
c) Two or three a day.

5. What is the most dangerous shark in the world?
a) The whale shark.
b) The great white shark.
c) The sea fox shark.

6. Do all sharks lay eggs?
a) Yes.
b) No. Some lay eggs and others give birth to live young.
c) None of them lay eggs.

The answers to SHARK SECRETS questions are on page 32.

GLOSSARY

ampullae of Lorenzini: a feature in a shark's body that enables it to detect weak electrical fields. Electricity is detected through pores near the bottom of a shark's snout that lead to jelly-filled sacs known as the ampullae of Lorenzini. All creatures have an electrical field, so these sense organs help a shark find and follow its prey.

anti-shark nets: fishing nets hung from buoys along a coast where sharks are common. Since 1937, Australia has used anti-shark nets to protect its beaches from sharks.

camouflage: the way a shark or some other animal or plant blends in and disguises itself with its surroundings by looking the same through color or texture. Some sharks have colored markings that allow them to sit at the bottom of the ocean floor and wait undetected.

carnivores: meat-eating animals. All sharks are carnivores, from the great white that eats large animals, to the basking shark that eats very tiny animals.

cartilage: an elastic substance that helps hold bones in place at the joints. Sharks, rays, and skates have skeletons made of cartilage.

caudal fin: the fin at the top of a shark's tail that adds speed and thrust to a shark's propulsion.

dimorphism: visible biological differences between male and female animals of the same species. For instance, female sharks are often larger than male sharks.

dorsal fin: the part of a shark's body that is seen above the water when the shark swims near the surface. This fin helps the shark keep its balance.

food chain: the name given to the delicate feeding cycle of all living creatures. Some animals and plants are food for other animals, those animals are food for other animals, and so on.

fusiform: a shape that is tapered at both ends.

gastric juices: digestive fluids that help dissolve food.

gills: the breathing organs in all fish, also known as the branchiae. Water enters the body through the gill slits and goes to the nearby gills. Here oxygen is removed by the bloodstream. The water then leaves through the gill slits.

invertebrates: any animals that do not have a spinal column. Invertebrates can be as small as a tiny shrimp or as large as a giant squid.

lateral lines: sensory organs near the shark's snout and along its entire body. These help the shark detect motion and vibrations in the water.

loin: the part of the side and back of an animal that is between the ribs and the hips.

marine: of or related to the sea. Marine life must live in the salt water of the oceans and seas.

oviparous: having the ability to produce eggs that hatch outside the body. Many female sharks are oviparous.

pectoral fins: fins similar to the wings of an airplane that guide sharks up and down. They do not move from side-to-side, but rather tilt forward or backward.

phytoplankton: tiny plants that float in the water. This plant life is a vital part of the food chain for many sea animals.

polar: relating to those regions of Earth that are very cold and icy. The elements of polar regions, such as the North Pole and the South Pole, are harsh to humans, but many animals live in these areas, including some species of sharks.

propulsion: the action of going forward and moving. A shark propels itself through the water by moving its caudal fin, or tail fin.

stabilizer: a structure, like a fin, that prevents excessive rolling. Ships and airplanes use fin-shaped devices as stabilizers.

tropical: belonging to the tropics, or the region centered on the equator and lying between the Tropic of Cancer (23.5 degrees south of the equator) and the Tropic of Capricorn (23.5 degrees north of the equator). This region is typically very hot and humid.

vertebral column: the spinal column, or backbone, which is made up of many small segments of cartilage or bone. Animals with backbones are called vertebrates.

voracious: eager to consume great amounts of food; having an unsatisfied appetite.

zooplankton: tiny animals that float in the water. Certain species of sharks, such as the basking and whale sharks, dine exclusively on these creatures. The sharks are equipped with special straining gills that scoop and collect the animals from the water.

ACTIVITIES

◆ Sharks are considered the most efficient hunters. Why are sharks so good at attacking their prey? Compare the hunting habits of sharks with other animals that are considered great hunters, such as lions, eagles, and even humans. What does a shark have that makes it such a good hunter that other creatures do not? After your research, do you still think sharks are the most dangerous hunters?

◆ Some species of sharks are endangered or are in danger of becoming so. Are sharks a bigger threat to humans, or are humans a bigger threat to sharks? Find out which species of sharks are commonly hunted by humans and why. Which cultures consider eating sharks a delicacy? What other reasons are there for hunting sharks? Which sharks are in the most danger of becoming extinct, and what is being done to save them?

MORE BOOKS TO READ

The Great White Shark. Carl R. Green and William R. Sanford
   (Macmillan Children's Book Group)
The Sea World Book of Sharks. Eve Bunting (Harcourt Brace)
Shark. Michael Chinery (Troll Associates)
Shark. Miranda MacQuitty (Knopf Books for Young Readers)
Sharks. (Running Press)
Sharks. Sheena Coupe (Facts on File)
Sharks. Gary Lopez (Child's World)
Sharks. Denny Robson (Watts)
Sharks. Lee Server (Outlet Book Company)
Sharks: Challengers of the Deep. Mary M. Cerullo (Dutton)
Sharks: The Perfect Predators. Howard Hall (Blake Publishing)
Watch Out For Sharks! Caroline Arnold (Houghton Mifflin)

VIDEOS

The Shark: Maneater or Myth? (Britannica Films)
Shark Chronicles. (ABC Video)
Shark Hunter. (Questar Home Video, Karol Video)
Sharks. (Vestron Video, Increase/SilverMine Video)
Sharks: Predators in Peril. (Fast Forward)

PLACES TO VISIT

Vancouver Aquarium
In Stanley Park
Vancouver, British
   Columbia
V6B 3X8

**Aquarium of the
   Americas**
1 Canal Street
New Orleans, LA 70178

**Sea World on the
   Gold Coast**
Sea World Drive Spit
Surfers Paradise
Queensland, Australia
4217

The Aquarium
Marine Parade
Napier, New Zealand

John G. Shedd Aquarium
1200 South Lake Shore
   Drive
Chicago, IL 60605

Sea World
1720 South Shores Road
San Diego, CA 92109

INDEX

Answers to SHARK SECRETS questions:
1. **b**
2. **c**
3. **a**
4. **a**
5. **b**
6. **b**